M000073244

POETRY
— TO —
CALM
YOUR
SOUL

For Vida, Lila and Ali

POETRY
— TO —
CALM
YOUR
SOUL

Compiled by Mimi Khalvati

MQP

Contents

Preface

The root of the word calm, in the Greek and Latin words for heat, suggests that apex of quiet and stillness the sun imposes on us in the middle of a burning day. The poems in this anthology all rest in a moment of suspension from struggle. They talk to the reader and to each other as neighbors might talk quietly in their houses or on the street, on the other side of a wall, sometimes laughing, commiserating, sharing the moment.

These voices are locked in the age-old arguments between love and grief, the heart and mind, soul and self. They love the world they live in, they mourn its passing, they accept the fact of death. Above all, they draw solace from the natural world and its capacity for change and renewal, and find in nature the will to keep faith. Flowers, trees, seas and stars, the most traditional of lyric emblems, shine as if they'd never shone before, and celebrate the eternal. Imagined worlds, spiritual or divine, also spread their leaves while others tell us "what we need is here."

The walls between the poems are thin: each poem seems to overhear the one before and to carry on a conversation. One lullaby is answered with another; one snow melts into a deeper snow; one fall from Paradise is caught in the hands of another. Seamlessness engenders a feeling of calm and enacts the very condition the poems strive for—of connection. The poems converse from sunrise through moonrise and on into darkness. While the pages turn, the seasons also turn and the cycle of birth, death, renewal, in all its calm inevitability, completes itself. Here are poems where the battle has been fought and the grace of love, peace and the brightness of the soul are, if only for this moment, felt and shared.

Mimi Khalvati

Into the hour

I have come into the hour of a white feeling.
Grief's surgery is over and I wear
The scar of my remorse and of my feeling.

I have come into a sudden sunlit hour
When ghosts are scared to corners. I have come
Into the time when grief begins to flower

Into a new love. It had filled my room
Long before I recognized it. Now
I speak its name. Grief finds its good way home.

The apple-blossom's handsome on the bough
And Paradise spreads round. I touch its grass.
I want to celebrate but don't know how.

I need not speak though everyone I pass
Stares at me kindly. I would put my hand
Into their hands. Now I have lost my loss

In some way I may later understand.
I hear the singing of the summer grass.
And love, I find, has no considered end,

Nor is it subject to the wilderness
Which follows death. I am not traitor to
A person or a memory. I trace

Behind that love another which is running
Around, ahead. I need not ask its meaning.

Elizabeth Jennings

The house was quiet
and the world was calm

The house was quiet and the world was calm.
The reader became the book; and summer night

Was like the conscious being of the book.
The house was quiet and the world was calm.

The words were spoken as if there was no book,
Except that the reader leaned above the page,

Wanted to lean, wanted much most to be
The scholar to whom his book is true, to whom

The summer night is like a perfection of thought.
The house was quiet because it had to be.

The quiet was part of the meaning, part of the mind:
The access of perfection to the page.

And the world was calm. The truth in a calm world,
In which there is no other meaning, itself

Is calm, itself is summer and night, itself
Is the reader leaning late and reading there.

Wallace Stevens

Sleeping on the ceiling

It is so peaceful on the ceiling!
It is the Place de la Concorde.
The little crystal chandelier
is off, the fountain is in the dark.
Not a soul is in the park.

Below, where the wallpaper is peeling,
the Jardin des Plantes has locked its gates.
Those photographs are animals.
The mighty flowers and foliage rustle;
under the leaves the insects tunnel.

We must go under the wallpaper
to meet the insect-gladiator,
to battle with a net and trident,
and leave the fountain and the square.
But oh, that we could sleep up there…

Elizabeth Bishop

Staying at Ed's place

I like being in your apartment and not disturbing
        anything,
as in the woods I wouldn't want to move a tree,
or change the play of sun and shadow on the ground.

The yellow kitchen stool belongs right there
against white plaster. I haven't used your purple trowel
because I like the accidental cleft of shade you left in it.

At your small six-sided table, covered with mysterious
dents in the wood like a dartboard, I drink my coffee
from your brown mug. I look into the clearing

of your high front room, where sunlight slopes through
        bare
window squares. Your Afghanistan hammock, a man-
        sized cocoon
slung from wall to wall, your narrow desk and typewriter

are the only furniture. Each morning the light from the
        east
douses me, where, with folded legs, I sit in your meadow,
a casual spread of brilliant carpets. Like a cat or dog

I take a roll, then, stretched out flat
in the center of color and pattern, I listen
to the remote growl of trucks over cobbles on Bethune
street below.

When I open my eyes I discover the peaceful blank of the
    ceiling.
Its old paint layered surface is moonwhite
and trackless, like the Sea – of Tranquillity.

May Swenson

Snow water

A fastidious brewer of tea, a tea
Connoisseur as well as a poet,
I modestly request on my sixtieth
Birthday a gift of snow water.

Tea steam and ink stains. Single-
Mindedly I scald my teapot and
Measure out some Silver Needles Tea,
Enough for a second steeping.

Other favourites include Clear
Distance and Eyebrows of Longevity
Or, from precarious mountain peaks,
Cloud Mist Tea (quite delectable)

Which competent monkeys harvest
Filling their baskets with choice leaves
And bringing them down to where I wait
With my crock of snow water.

Michael Longley

Tea mind

Even as a child I could
induce it at will.
I'd go to where the big rocks

stayed cold in the woods all summer,
and tea mind would come to me

like water over stones, pool to pool,
and in that way I taught myself to think.
Green teas are my favorites, especially

the basket-fired Japanese ones
that smell of baled hay.

Thank you, makers of this tea.
Because of you my mind is still tonight,
transparent, a leaf in air.

Now it rides a subtle current.
Now it can finally disappear.

Chase Twichell

Everything is going to be all right

How should I not be glad to contemplate
the clouds clearing beyond the dormer window
and a high tide reflected on the ceiling?
There will be dying, there will be dying,
but there is no need to go into that.
The lines flow from the hand unbidden
and the hidden source is the watchful heart.
The sun rises in spite of everything
and the far cities are beautiful and bright.
I lie here in a riot of sunlight
watching the day break and the clouds flying.
Everything is going to be all right.

Derek Mahon

Blue grapes

Eating blue grapes
      near the window
   and looking out
      at the snow-covered valley.
For a moment, the deep world
      gazing back. Then a blue jay
   scatters snow from a bough.
No world, no meeting. Only
     tremors, sweetness
           on the tongue.

Tess Gallagher

The song

From somewhere
a calm musical note arrives.
You balance it on your tongue,
a single ripe grape,
till your whole body glistens.
In the space between breaths
you apply it to any wound
and the wound heals.

Soon the nights will lengthen,
you will lean into the year
humming like a saw.
You will fill the lamps with kerosene,
knowing somewhere a line breaks,
a city goes black,
people dig for candles in the bottom drawer.
You will be ready. You will use the song like a match.
It will fill your rooms
opening rooms of its own
so you sing, I did not know
my house was this large.

Naomi Shihab Nye

The gateway

Now the heart sings with all its thousand voices
To hear this city of cells, my body, sing.
The tree through the stiff clay at long last forces
Its thin strong roots and taps the secret spring.

And the sweet waters without intermission
Climb to the tips of its green tenement;
The breasts have borne the grace of their possession,
The lips have felt the pressure of content.

Here I come home: in this expected country
They know my name and speak it with delight.
I am the dream and you the gates of entry,
The means by which I waken into light.

A. D. Hope

Sudden light

I have been here before,
    But when or how I cannot tell:
I know the grass beyond the door,
    The sweet keen smell,
The sighing sound, the lights around the shore.

You have been mine before, –
    How long ago I may not know:
But just when at that swallow's soar
    Your neck turned so,
Some veil did fall, – I knew it all of yore.

Has this been thus before?
    And shall not thus time's eddying flight
Still with our lives our love restore
    In death's despite,
And day and night yield one delight once more?

Dante Gabriel Rossetti

I leave this at your ear

for Nessie Dunsmuir

I leave this at your ear for when you wake,
A creature in its abstract cage asleep.
Your dreams blindfold you by the light they make.

The owl called from the naked-woman tree
As I came down by the Kyle farm to hear
Your house silent by the speaking sea.

I have come late but I have come before
Later with slaked steps from stone to stone
To hope to find you listening for the door.

I stand in the ticking room. My dear, I take
A moth kiss from your breath. The shore gulls cry.
I leave this at your ear for when you wake.

W. S. Graham

Winter sunrise

It is early morning within this room: without,
Dark and damp: without and within, stillness
Waiting for day: not a sound but a listening air.

Yellow jasmine, delicate on stiff branches
Stands in a Tuscan pot to delight the eye
In spare December's patient nakedness.

Suddenly, softly, as if at a breath breathed
On the pale wall, a magical apparition,
The shadow of the jasmine, branch and blossom!

It was not there, it is there, in a perfect image;
And all is changed. It is like a memory lost
Returning without a reason into the mind;

And it seems to me that the beauty of the shadow
Is more beautiful than the flower; a strange beauty,
Pencilled and silently deepening to distinctness.

As a memory stealing out of the mind's slumber,
A memory floating up from a dark water,
Can be more beautiful than the thing remembered.

Laurence Binyon

On a clothesline between two pines

Summer and the cool of early morning,
a faded version of the moon
still in the sky,
then just the driftwood-gray clothespins
and the white of the towel
forgotton on the line,
the night's damp still in it,
and not much else
except that somehow we'd crossed over,
opened our eyes
or splashed our faces at the sink,
that there are stones to touch
and thoughts we couldn't,
and now unfolding chairs:
canvas snapping into place,
wooden legs settling
into sand under us,
that all of this could happen,
that it could stop,
not just dreams, but sleep itself,
rain, mist, evaporation.

Jane O. Wayne

Trees in the garden

Ah in the thunder air
How still the trees are!

And the lime-tree, lovely and tall, every leaf silent
Hardly looses even a last breath of perfume.

And the ghostly, creamy colored little tree of leaves
White, ivory white among the rambling greens
How evanescent, variegated elder, she hesitates on the
    green grass
As if, in another moment, she would disappear
With all her grace of foam!

And the larch that is only a column, it goes up too tall to
    see:
And the balsam-pines that are blue with the grey-blue
    blueness of things from the sea,
And the young copper beech, its leaves red-rosy at the ends
How still they are together, they stand so still
In the thunder air, all strangers to one another
As the green grass glows upwards, strangers in the silent
    garden.

D. H. Lawrence

Consider the grass growing

Consider the grass growing
As it grew last year and the year before,
Cool about the ankles like summer rivers,
When we walked on a May evening through the meadows
To watch the mare that was going to foal.

Patrick Kavanagh

A blessing

Just off the highway to Rochester, Minnesota,
Twilight bounds softly forth on the grass.
And the eyes of those two Indian ponies
Darken with kindness.
They have come gladly out of the willows
To welcome my friend and me.
We step over the barbed wire into the pasture
Where they have been grazing all day, alone.
They ripple tensely, they can hardly contain their
     happiness
That we have come.
They bow shyly as wet swans. They love each other.
There is no loneliness like theirs.
At home once more,
They begin munching the young tufts of spring in the
     darkness.
I would like to hold the slenderer one in my arms,
For she has walked over to me
And nuzzled my left hand.
She is black and white,
Her mane falls wild on her forehead,
And the light breeze moves me to caress her long ear
That is delicate as the skin over a girl's wrist.
Suddenly I realize
That if I stepped out of my body I would break
Into blossom.

James Wright

Break

We put the puzzle together piece
by piece, loving how one curved
notch fits so sweetly with another.
A yellow smudge becomes
the brush of a broom, and two blue arms
fill in the last of the sky.
We patch together porch swings and autumn
trees, matching gold to gold. We hold
the eyes of deer in our palms, a pair
of brown shoes. We do this as the child
circles her room, impatient
with her blossoming, tired
of the neat house, the made bed,
the good food. We let her brood
as we shuffle through the pieces,
setting each one into place with a satisfied
tap, our backs turned for a few hours
to a world that is crumbling, a sky
that is falling, the pieces
we are required to return to.

Dorianne Laux

from The Georgics Book IV

I remember once beneath the battlements of Oebalia,
Where dark Galaesus waters the golden fields of corn,
I saw an old man, a Corycian, who owned a few poor acres
Of land once derelict, useless for arable,
No good for grazing, unfit for the cultivation of vines.
But he laid out a kitchen garden in rows amid the
  brushwood,
Bordering it with white lilies, verbena, small-seeded
  poppy.
He was happy as a king. He could go indoors at night
to a table heaped with dainties he never had to buy.
His the first rose of spring, the earliest apples in autumn:
And when grim winter still was splitting the rocks with
  cold
And holding the watercourses with curb of ice, already
That man would be cutting his soft-haired hyacinths,
  complaining
Of summer's backwardness and the west winds slow to
  come.
His bees were the first to breed,
Enriching him with huge swarms: he squeezed the frothy
  honey
Before anyone else from the combs: he had limes and a
  wealth of pine trees:
And all the early blossom, that clothed his trees with
  promise
Of an apple crop, by autumn had come to maturity.

He had a gift, too, for transplanting in rows the far-grown
  elm,
The hardwood pear, the blackthorn bearing its weight of
  sloes,
And the plane that already offered a pleasant shade for
  drinking.
But these are matters the strict scope of my theme forbids
  me:
I must pass them by, and leave them for later men to
  enlarge on.

Virgil
(Translated from the Latin by C. Day Lewis)

Apple blossom

The first blossom was the best blossom
For the child who never had seen an orchard;
For the youth whom whisky had led astray
The morning after was the first day.

The first apple was the best apple
For Adam before he heard the sentence;
When the flaming sword endorsed the Fall
The trees were his to plant for all.

The first ocean was the best ocean
For the child from streets of doubt and litter;
For the youth for whom the skies unfurled
His first love was his first world.

But the first verdict seemed the worst verdict
When Adam and Eve were expelled from Eden;
Yet when the bitter gates clanged to
The sky beyond was just as blue.

For the next ocean is the first ocean
And the last ocean is the first ocean
And, however often the sun may rise,
A new thing dawns upon our eyes.

For the last blossom is the first blossom
And the first blossom is the best blossom
And when from Eden we take our way
The morning after is the first day.

Louis MacNeice

Autumn

The leaves are falling, falling as if from far up,
as if orchards were dying high in space.
Each leaf falls as if it were motioning "no."

And tonight the heavy earth is falling
away from all the other stars in the loneliness.

We're all falling. This hand here is falling.
And look at the other one…it's in them all.

And yet there is Someone, whose hands
infinitely calm, hold up all this falling.

Rainer Maria Rilke
(Translated from the German by Robert Bly)

'I dwell in possibility –'

I dwell in Possibility –
A fairer House than Prose –
More numerous of Windows –
Superior – for Doors –

Of Chambers as the Cedars –
Impregnable of Eye –
And for an Everlasting Roof
The Gambrels of the Sky

Of Visitors – the fairest –
For Occupation – This –
The spreading wide my narrow Hands
To gather Paradise –

Emily Dickinson

from The Garden

What wondrous life is this I lead!
Ripe apples drop about my head;
The luscious clusters of the vine
Upon my mouth do crush their wine;
The nectarene, and curious peach,
Into my hands themselves do reach;
Stumbling on melons, as I pass,
Ensnared with flowers, I fall on grass.

Meanwhile the mind, from pleasures less,
Withdraws into its happiness:
The mind, that ocean where each kind
Does straight its own resemblance find;
Yet it creates, transcending these,
Far other worlds, and other seas,
Annihilating all that's made
To a green thought in a green shade.

Andrew Marvell

Question and answer in the mountains

They ask me why I live in the green mountains.
I smile and don't reply; my heart's at ease.
Peach blossoms flow downstream, leaving no trace –
And there are other earths and skies than these.

Li Po
(Translated from the Chinese by Vikram Seth)

The lake isle of Innisfree

I will arise and go now, and go to Innisfree,
And a small cabin build there, of clay and wattles made:
Nine bean-rows will I have there, a hive for the honey-bee,
And live alone in the bee-loud glade.

And I shall have some peace there, for peace comes
dropping
    slow,
Dropping from the veils of the morning to where the
cricket
    sings;
There midnight's all a glimmer, and noon a purple glow,
And evening full of the linnet's wings.

I will arise and go now, for always night and day
I hear lake water lapping with low sounds by the shore;
While I stand on the roadway, or on the pavements gray,
I hear it in the deep heart's core.

W. B. Yeats

Gorgeous – yet another Brighton poem

The summer's here.
Down to the beach
to swim and lounge and swim again.
Gorgeous bodies young and old.
Me too. Just gorgeous. Just feeling good
and happy and so at ease in the world.

And come early evening a red sun setting,
the sea all silky,
small gentle surges along its near still surface.

And later
the new moon hung over the sea,
a stippled band of gold across the black water,
tiger's eye.

I walk home.
The air so soft and warm,
like fur brushing my body.

The dictionary says
"**gorgeous** – adorned with rich and brilliant colors,
sumptuously splendid, showy, magnificent, dazzling."

That's right.

Lee Harwood

Phases of the moon

Once upon a time I heard
That the flying moon was a Phoenix bird;
Thus she sails through windy skies,
Thus in the willow's arms she lies;
Turn to the East or turn to the West
In many trees she makes her nest.
When she's but a pearly thread
Look among birch leaves overhead;
When she dies in yellow smoke
Look in a thunder-smitten oak;
But in May when the moon is full,
Bright as water and white as wool,
Look for her where she loves to be,
Asleep in a high magnolia tree.

Elinor Wylie

Hut among the bamboos

Sitting alone
 in the hush of the bamboo grove
I thrum my lute
 and whistle lingering notes.
In the secrecy of the wood
 no one can hear –
Only the clear moon
 comes to shine on me.

Wang Wei
(translated from the Chinese)

To the moon

Now that the year has come full circle,
I remember climbing this hill, heartbroken,
To gaze up at the graceful sight of you,
And how you hung then above those woods
As you do tonight, bathing them in brightness.
But at that time your face seemed nothing
But a cloudy shimmering through my tears,
So wretched was the life I led: and lead still…
Nothing changes, moon of my delight. Yet
I find pleasure in recollection, in calling back
My season of grief: when one is young,
And hope is a long road, memory
A short one, how welcome then
The remembrance of things past – no matter
How sad, and the heart still grieving.

Giacomo Leopardi
(Translated from the Italian by Eamon Grennan)

Remember

Remember me when I am gone away,
  Gone far away into the silent land;
  When you can no more hold me by the hand,
Nor I half turn to go yet turning stay.
Remember me when no more day by day
  You tell me of our future that you plann'd:
  Only remember me; you understand
It will be late to counsel then or pray.
Yet if you should forget me for a while
  And afterwards remember, do not grieve:
  For if the darkness and corruption leave
  A vestige of the thoughts that once I had,
Better by far you should forget and smile
  Than that you should remember and be sad.

Christina Rossetti

from When one has lived a long time alone

When one has lived a long time alone,
one refrains from swatting the fly
and lets him go, and one hesitates to strike
the mosquito, though more than willing to slap
the flesh under her, and one lifts the toad
from the pit too deep to hop out of
and carries him to the grass, without minding
the poisoned urine he slicks his body with,
and one envelops, in a towel, the swift
who fell down the chimney and knocks herself
against window glass and releases her outside
and watches her fly free, a life line flung at reality,
when one has lived a long time alone.

Galway Kinnell

Lying

He puts his brush to the canvas,
with one quick stroke
unfolds a bird from the sky.
Steps back, considers.
Takes pity.
Unfolds another.

Jane Hirshfield

Full moon and little Frieda

A cool small evening shrunk to a dog bark and the clank
    of a bucket –

And you listening.
A spider's web, tense for the dew's touch.
A pail lifted, still and brimming – mirror
To tempt a first star to a tremor.

Cows are going home in the lane there, looping the hedges
    with their warm wreaths of breath –
A dark river of blood, many boulders,
Balancing unspilled milk.

'Moon!' you cry suddenly, 'Moon! Moon!'

The moon has stepped back like an artist gazing amazed
    at a work

That points at him amazed.

Ted Hughes

How I discovered poetry

It was like soul-kissing, the way the words
filled my mouth as Mrs. Purdy read from her desk.
All the other kids zoned an hour ahead to 3:15,
but Mrs. Purdy and I wandered lonely as clouds borne
by a breeze off Mount Parnassus. She must have seen
the darkest eyes in the room brim: The next day
she gave me a poem she'd chosen especially for me
to read to the all except for me white class.
She smiled when she told me to read it, smiled harder,
said oh yes I could. She smiled harder and harder
until I stood and opened my mouth to banjo playing
darkies, pickaninnies, disses and dats. When I finished
my classmates stared at the floor. We walked silent
to the buses, awed by the power of words.

Marilyn Nelson

Light

I live for books
and light to read them in.
       Waterlilies
reaching up
from the depths of the pond
algae dark,
the frog loves a jell of
blue-green water,
       the bud
scales
a rope of stem,
then floats in sunshine. Like soap
in the morning bath.
This book I read
floats in my hand like a waterlily
coming out of the nutrient waters
of thought
and light shines on us both,
the morning's breviary.

Diane Wakoski

What is poetry

The medieval town, with frieze
Of boy scouts from Nagoya? The snow

That came when we wanted it to snow?
Beautiful images? Trying to avoid

Ideas, as in this poem? But we
Go back to them as to a wife, leaving

The mistress we desire? Now they
Will have to believe it

As we believe it. In school
All the thought got combed out:

What was left was like a field.
Shut your eyes, and you can feel it for miles around.

Now open them on a thin vertical path.
It might give us – what?– some flowers soon?

John Ashbery

'Flowers come as a gift'

Flowers come as a gift
    sent down from Paradise
And in their presence man
    lives with a kinder heart –
O Flower-Seller selling
    flowers for silver, what
Will silver buy more lovely
    than that with which you part?

Kesa'i
(Translated from the Persian by Dick Davis)

'A thing of beauty is a joy for ever:'

A thing of beauty is a joy for ever:
Its loveliness increases; it will never
Pass into nothingness; but will still keep
A bower quiet for us, and a sleep
Full of sweet dreams, and health, and quiet breathing.
Therefore, on every morrow, are we wreathing
A flowery band to bind us to the earth,
Spite of despondence, of the inhuman dearth
Of noble natures, of the gloomy days,
Of all the unhealthy and o'er-darkened ways
Made for our searching: yes, in spite of all,
Some shape of beauty moves away the pall
From our dark spirits.

John Keats

'When I gathered flowers'

When I gathered flowers
For my girl
From the top of the plum tree,
The lower branches
Drenched me with dew.

Kakinomoto no Hitomaro
(Translated from the Japanese by Kenneth Rexroth)

Ah! Sun-flower

Ah, Sun-flower, weary of time,
Who countest the steps of the Sun,
Seeking after that sweet golden clime
Where the traveller's journey is done:

Where the Youth pined away with desire,
And the pale Virgin shrouded in snow
Arise from their graves, and aspire
Where my Sun-flower wishes to go.

William Blake

Flowers by the sea

When over the flowery, sharp pasture's
edge, unseen, the salt ocean

lifts its form – chicory and daisies
tied, released, seem hardly flowers alone

but color and the movement – or the shape
perhaps – of restlessness, whereas

the sea is circled and sways
peacefully upon its plantlike stem

William Carlos Williams

Springing

In a skiff on a sunrisen lake we are watchers.

Swimming aimlessly is luxury just as walking
loudly up a shallow stream is.

As we lean over the deep well, we whisper.

Friends at hearths are drawn to the one warm air;
strangers meet on beaches drawn to the one wet sea.

What wd it be to be water, one body of water
(what water is is another mystery) (We are
water divided.) It wd be a self without walls,
with surface tension, specific gravity a local
exchange between bedrock and cloud of falling and rising,
rising to fall, falling to rise.

Marie Ponsot

from Lines written a few miles above Tintern Abbey, on revisiting the banks of the Wye, July 13, 1798

Five years have passed; five summers, with the length
Of five long winters! and again I hear
These waters, rolling from their mountain-springs
With a sweet inland murmur. – Once again
Do I behold these steep and lofty cliffs,
Which on a wild secluded scene impress
Thoughts of more deep seclusion; and connect
The landscape with the quiet of the sky.
The day is come when I again repose
Here, under this dark sycamore, and view
These plots of cottage-ground, these orchard-tufts,
Which, at this season, with their unripe fruits,
Among the woods and copses lose themselves,
Nor, with their green and simple hue, disturb
The wild green landscape. Once again I see
these hedge-rows, hardly hedge-rows, little lines
Of sportive wood run wild; these pastoral farms
Green to the very door; and wreathes of smoke
Sent up, in silence, from among the trees,
With some uncertain notice, as might seem,
Of vagrant dwellers in the houseless woods,
Or of some hermit's cave, where by his fire
The hermit sits alone.

        Though absent long,
These forms of beauty have not been to me,
As is a landscape to a blind man's eye:
But oft, in lonely rooms, and mid the din
Of towns and cities, I have owed to them,
In hours of weariness, sensations sweet,
Felt in the blood, and felt along the heart,
And passing even into my purer mind
With tranquil restoration: – feelings too
Of unremembered pleasure; such, perhaps,
As may have had no trivial influence
On that best portion of a good man's life;
His little, nameless, unremembered acts
Of kindness and of love. Nor less, I trust,
To them I may have owed another gift,
Of aspect more sublime; that blessed mood,
In which the burthen of the mystery,
In which the heavy and the weary weight
Of all this unintelligible world
Is lightened: – that serene and blessed mood,
In which the affections gently lead us on,
Until, the breath of this corporeal frame,
And even the motion of our human blood
Almost suspended, we are laid asleep
In body, and become a living soul:
While with an eye made quiet by the power
Of harmony, and the deep power of joy,
We see into the life of things.

William Wordsworth

Calm

The lake, gone beyond thinking, slips out of itself,
casts reflections across skirts of fir

greening the shore, making of their wind-still study
a flicker and slide, the way souls move, ichorous,
    transparent,

hovering near the flesh before they go. I want the green
    under green,
the thought inside the thought, the one deep down and
    cold,

raveling its divination in the dark. Are there gods without
    thirst?
Who need no slaking? Ungathered, the water's blank and
    beautiful,

intricately wrought. No one knows where mind and body
come together, that clean join thin fingerlings slip through.

Lorna Crozier

Some questions you might ask

Is the soul solid, like iron?
Or is it tender and breakable, like
the wings of a moth in the beak of the owl?
Who has it, and who doesn't?
I keep looking around me.
The face of the moose is as sad
as the face of Jesus.
The swan opens her white wings slowly.
In the fall, the black bear carries leaves into the darkness.
One question leads to another.
Does it have a shape? Like an iceberg?
Like the eye of a hummingbird?
Does it have one lung, like the snake and the scallop?
Why should I have it, and not the anteater
who loves her children?
Why should I have it, and not the camel?
Come to think of it, what about the maple trees?
What about the blue iris?
What about all the little stones, sitting alone in the
    moonlight?
What about roses, and lemons, and their shining leaves?
What about the grass?

Mary Oliver

Apple tree

No choice for the apple tree.
And after the surgeon's chainsaw,
from one stubborn root

two plumes of tree now leaf
and even blossom, sky's
cool blue between them,

whereas on my left hand
not a single lifeline
but three deep equal

channels –
        O my soul,
it is not a small thing,
to have made from three

this one, this one life.

Ellen Bryant Voigt

Summer farm

Straws like tame lightnings lie about the grass
And hang zigzag on hedges. Green as glass
The water in the water-trough shines.
Nine ducks go wobbling by in two straight lines.

A hen stares at nothing with one eye,
Then picks it up. Out of an empty sky
A swallow falls and, flickering through
The barn, dives up again into the dizzy blue.

I lie, not thinking, in the cool, soft grass,
Afraid of where a thought might take me – as
This grasshopper with plated face
Unfolds his legs and finds himself in space.

Self under self, a pile of selves I stand
Threaded on time, and with metaphysic hand
Lift the farm like a lid and see
Farm within farm, and in the center, me.

Norman MacCaig

A noiseless patient spider

A noiseless patient spider,
I marked where on a little promontory it stood isolated,
Marked how to explore the vacant vast surrounding,
It launched forth filament, filament, filament, out of itself,
Ever unreeling them, ever tirelessly speeding them.

And you O my soul where you stand,
Surrounded, detached, in measureless oceans of space,
Ceaselessly musing, venturing, throwing, seeking the
    spheres to connect them,
Till the bridge you will need be formed, till the ductile
    anchor hold,
Till the gossamer thread you fling catch somewhere, O
    my soul.

Walt Whitman

My star

All that I know
Of a certain star
Is, it can throw
  (Like the angled spar)
 Now a dart of red,
  Now a dart of blue;
 Till my friends have said
  They would fain see, too,
My star that dartles the red and the blue!
Then it stops like a bird; like a flower, hangs furled:
  They must solace themselves with the Saturn
    above it.
What matter to me if their star is a world?
  Mine has opened its soul to me; therefore I love
    it.

Robert Browning

The more loving one

Looking up at the stars, I know quite well
That, for all they care, I can go to hell,
But on earth indifference is the least
We have to dread from man or beast.

How should we like it were stars to burn
With a passion for us we could not return?
If equal affection cannot be,
Let the more loving one be me.

Admirer as I think I am
Of stars that do not give a damn,
I cannot, now I see them, say
I missed one terribly all day.

Were all stars to disappear or die,
I should learn to look at an empty sky
And feel its total dark sublime,
Though this might take me a little time.

W. H. Auden

Sonnet

Well, she told me I had an aura. "What?" I said.
"An aura," she said. "I heered you," I said, "but
you ain't significating." "What I mean, you got
this fuzzy light like, all around your head,
same as Nell the epelectric when she's nigh read-
y to have a fit, only you ain't having no fit."
"Why, that's a fact," I said, "and I ain't about
to neither. I reckon it's more like that dead
rotten fir stump by the edge of the swamp on misty
nights long about cucumber-blossoming time
when the foxfire's flickering round." "I be goddam
if that's it," she said. "Why, you ain't but sixty-
nine, you ain't a-rotting yet. What I say
is you got a goddamn naura." "OK," I said. "OK."

Hayden Carruth

The giantess

Long, long ago, when Nature had some zest
And mothered monsters and was not effete,
I would have loved to live with a young giantess,
Like a voluptuous cat at a queen's feet.

Oh to have watched her soul begin to flower! – her size
Increasing wantonly in dreadful games;

To guess from misty looks and swimming eyes
Her heart was brooding maybe some dark flame;

To cross her magnificent contours as I pleased;

Crawl on the slope of her enormous knees;

And sometimes, when unhealthy suns had laid
Her length across the landscape, dazed with heat,
To sleep untroubled in her breasts' warm shade,
Like a calm hamlet at a mountain's feet.

Charles Baudelaire
(*Translated from the French by Alistair Elliot*)

Song, from A Midsummer Night's Dream

You spotted snakes with double tongue,
Thorny hedgehogs, be not seen;
Newts and blind-worms, do no wrong,
Come not near our fairy queen.
Philomel with melody,
Sing in our sweet lullaby;
Lulla, lulla, lullaby; lulla lulla, lullaby;
Never harm
Nor spell nor charm
Come our lovely lady nigh.
So good night, with lullaby.
Weaving spiders, come not here;
Hence, you long-legg'd spinners, hence.
Beetles black, approach not near;
Worm nor snail do no offence.
Philomel with melody,
Sing in our sweet lullaby;
Lulla, lulla, lullaby; lulla, lulla, lullaby;
Never harm
Nor spell nor charm
Come our lovely lady nigh.
So good night, with lullaby.

William Shakespeare

Song, from The Tempest

Where the bee sucks, there suck I,

In a cowslip's bell I lie;

There I couch when owls do cry.

On the bat's back I do fly

After summer merrily.

Merrily, merrily, shall I live now,
Under the blossom that hangs on the bough.

William Shakespeare

Lullaby

Time to rest now; you have had
enough excitement for the time being.

Twilight, then early evening. Fireflies
in the room, flickering here and there, here and there,
and summer's deep sweetness filling the open window.

Don't think of these things anymore.
Listen to my breathing, your own breathing
like the fireflies, each small breath
a flare in which the world appears.

I've sung to you long enough in the summer night.
I'll win you over in the end; the world can't give you
this sustained vision.

You must be taught to love me. Human beings must be
        taught to love
silence and darkness.

Louise Glück

from **Frost at midnight**

The Frost performs its secret ministry,
Unhelped by any wind. The owlet's cry
Came loud – and hark, again! loud as before.
The inmates of my cottage, all at rest,
Have left me to that solitude, which suits
Abstruser musings: save that at my side
My cradled infant slumbers peacefully.
'Tis calm indeed! so calm, that it disturbs
And vexes meditation with its strange
And extreme silentness. Sea, hill, and wood,
This populous village! Sea, and hill, and wood,
With all the numberless goings-on of life,
Inaudible as dreams! the thin blue flame
Lies on my low-burnt fire, and quivers not;
Only that film, which fluttered on the grate,
Still flutters there, the sole unquiet thing.
Methinks, its motion in this hush of nature
Gives it dim sympathies with me who live,
Making it a companionable form,
Whose puny flaps and freaks the idling Spirit
By its own moods interprets, every where
Echo or mirror seeking of itself,
And makes a toy of Thought. (…)

Dear Babe, that sleepest cradled by my side,
Whose gentle breathings, heard in this deep calm,
Fill up the interspersèd vacancies
And momentary pauses of the thought!

My babe so beautiful! it thrills my heart
With tender gladness, thus to look at thee,
And think that thou shalt learn far other lore,
And in far other scenes! For I was reared
In the great city, pent 'mid cloisters dim,
And saw nought lovely but the sky and stars.
But thou, my babe! shalt wander like a breeze
By lakes and sandy shores, beneath the crags
Of ancient mountain, and beneath the clouds,
Which image in their bulk both lakes and shores
And mountain crags: so shalt thou see and hear
The lovely shapes and sounds intelligible
Of that eternal language, which thy God
Utters, who from eternity doth teach
Himself in all, and all things in himself.
Great universal Teacher! he shall mould
Thy spirit, and by giving make it ask.

    Therefore all seasons shall be sweet to thee,
Whether the summer clothe the general earth
With greenness, or the redbreast sit and sing
Betwixt the tufts of snow on the bare branch
Of mossy apple-tree, while the nigh thatch
Smokes in the sun-thaw; whether the eave-drops fall
Heard only in the trances of the blast,
Or if the secret ministry of frost
Shall hang them up in silent icicles,
Quietly shining to the quiet Moon.

Samuel Taylor Coleridge

Morning song

Love set you going like a fat gold watch.
The midwife slapped your footsoles, and your bald cry
Took its place among the elements.

Our voices echo, magnifying your arrival. New statue.
In a drafty museum, your nakedness
Shadows our safety. We stand round blankly as walls.

I'm no more your mother
Than the cloud that distils a mirror to reflect its own slow
Effacement at the wind's hand.

All night your moth-breath
Flickers among the flat pink roses. I wake to listen:
A far sea moves in my ear.

One cry, and I stumble from bed, cow-heavy and floral
In my Victorian nightgown.
Your mouth opens clean as a cat's. The window square

Whitens and swallows its dull stars. And now you try
Your handful of notes;
The clear vowels rise like balloons.

Sylvia Plath

Lullaby

AlirÔn, tira del cordÔn

Even now I sing the same lullabies
to my baby, the ones I learned
from my father, that came down
through Spanish time, cradlewood-time.

My boy caresses my face
with his soft hand, slowly
his hand passes across my face
in that instinctive way
babies have, almost not touching,
almost not caressing.

When I test the heat of the milk
on the inside of my wrist
it makes a row of tiny drops
and I think of the monks in Poblet
who are sprinkled with holy water
at vespers. How soft and unhurried
I must be for him.

This little boy has no cradle.
His father is a carpenter –
he will make him one
and I stop in the cradle-darkness
and listen to his breathing
in this deep country we live in together.

Jane Duran

Peace

My soul, there is a country
    Far beyond the stars,
Where stands a wingèd sentry
    All skilful in the wars:
There, above noise, and danger,
    Sweet Peace sits crowned with smiles,
And One born in a manger
    Commands the beauteous files.
He is thy gracious Friend,
    And – O my Soul awake! –
Did in pure love descend
    To die here for thy sake.
If thou canst get but thither,
    There grows the flower of Peace,
The Rose that cannot wither,
    Thy fortress, and thy ease.
Leave then thy foolish ranges;
    For none can thee secure
But One who never changes–
    Thy God, thy life, thy cure.

Henry Vaughan

Usk
from Landscapes

Do not suddenly break the branch, or
Hope to find
The white hart behind the white well.
Glance aside, not for lance, do not spell
Old enchantments. Let them sleep.
'Gently dip, but not too deep',
Lift your eyes
Where the roads dip and where the roads rise
Seek only there
Where the grey light meets the green air
The hermit's chapel, the pilgrim's prayer.

T. S. Eliot

Heaven-haven

A nun takes the veil

    I have desired to go
    Where springs not fail,
To fields where flies no sharp and sided hail
    And a few lilies blow.

    And I have asked to be
    Where no storms come,
Where the green swell is in the havens dumb,
    And out of the swing of the sea.

Gerard Manley Hopkins

Christmas party at the South Danbury church

    December twenty-first
we gather at the white Church festooned
    red and green, the tree flashing
green-red lights beside the altar.
    After the children of Sunday School
recite Scripture, sing songs,
    and scrape out solos,
they retire to dress for the finale,
    to perform the pageant
again: Mary and Joseph kneeling
    cradleside, Three Kings,
shepherds and shepherdesses. Their garments
    are bathrobes with mothholes,
cut down from the Church's ancestors.
    Standing short and long,
they stare in all directions for mothers,
    sisters and brothers,
giggling and waving in recognition,
    and at the South Danbury
Church, a moment before Santa
    arrives with her ho-hos
and bags of popcorn, in the half-dark
    of whole silence, God
enters the world as a newborn again.

Donald Hall

The oxen

Christmas Eve, and twelve of the clock.
　　'Now they are all on their knees,'
An elder said as we sat in a flock
　　By the embers in hearthside ease.

We pictured the meek mild creatures where
　　They dwelt in their strawy pen,
Nor did it occur to one of us there
　　To doubt they were kneeling then.

So fair a fancy few would weave
　　In these years! Yet, I feel,
If someone said on Christmas Eve,
　　'Come; see the oxen kneel

In the lonely barton by yonder coomb
　　Our childhood used to know,'
I should go with him in the gloom,
　　Hoping it might be so.

Thomas Hardy

The bright field

I have seen the sun break through
to illuminate a small field
for a while, and gone my way
and forgotten it. But that was the pearl
of great price, the one field that had
the treasure in it. I realize now
that I must give all that I have
to possess it. Life is not hurrying

on to a receding future, nor hankering after
an imagined past. It is the turning
aside like Moses to the miracle
of the lit bush, to a brightness
that seemed as transitory as your youth
once, but is the eternity that awaits you.

R. S. Thomas

In the fields

Lord when I look at lovely things which pass,
    Under old trees the shadow of young leaves
Dancing to please the wind along the grass,
    Or the gold stillness of the August sun on the August
      sheaves;
Can I believe there is a heavenlier world than this?
    And if there is
Will the heart of any everlasting thing
    Bring me these dreams that take my breath away?
They come at evening with the home-flying rooks and the
      scent of hay,
Over the fields. They come in spring.

Charlotte Mew

The trees

The trees are coming into leaf
Like something almost being said;
The recent buds relax and spread,
Their greenness is a kind of grief.

Is it that they are born again
And we grow old? No, they die too.
Their yearly trick of looking new
Is written down in rings of grain.

Yet still the unresting castles thresh
In fullgrown thickness every May.
Last year is dead, they seem to say,
Begin afresh, afresh, afresh.

Philip Larkin

The flower

    How fresh, O Lord, how sweet and clear
Are thy returns! ev'n as the flowers in spring;
    To which, besides their own demean,
The late-past frosts tributes of pleasure bring.
      Grief melts away
     Like snow in May,
  As if there were no such cold thing.

    Who would have thought my shrivelled heart
Could have recovered greenness? It was gone
    Quite underground; as flowers depart
To see their mother-root, when they have blown;
      Where they together
     All the hard weather,
Dead to the world, keep house unknown.

    These are thy wonders, Lord of power,
Killing and quick'ning, bringing down to hell
    And up to heaven in an hour;
Making a chiming of a passing-bell.
      We say amiss,
     This or that is:
Thy word is all, if we could spell.

    O that I once past changing were,
Fast in thy Paradise, where no flower can wither!
    Many a spring I shoot up fair,

Off'ring at heav'n, growing and groaning thither:
                    Nor doth my flower
                    Want a spring-shower,
          My sins and I joining together:

          But while I grow in a straight line,
Still upwards bent, as if heav'n were mine own,
          Thy anger comes, and I decline:
What frost to that? what pole is not the zone,
                    Where all things burn,
                    When thou dost turn,
          And the least frown of thine is shown?

          And now in age I bud again,
After so many deaths I live and write;
          I once more smell the dew and rain,
And relish versing: O my only light,
                    It cannot be
                    That I am he
          On whom thy tempests fell all night.

          These are thy wonders, Lord of love;
To make us see we are but flowers that glide:
          Which when we once can find and prove,
Thou hast a garden for us, where to bide.
                    Who would be more
                    Swelling through store,
          Forfeit their Paradise by their pride.

George Herbert

'All nature has a feeling'

All nature has a feeling: woods, fields, brooks
Are life eternal: and in silence they
Speak happiness beyond the reach of books;
There's nothing mortal in them; their decay
Is the green life of change; to pass away
And come again in blooms revivified.
Its birth was heaven, eternal is its stay,
And with the sun and moon shall still abide
Beneath their day and night and heaven wide.

John Clare

'The annals say...'
from Lightenings

The annals say: when the monks of Clonmacnoise
Were all at prayers inside the oratory
A ship appeared above them in the air.

The anchor dragged along behind so deep
It hooked itself into the altar rails
And then, as the big hull rocked to a standstill,

A crewman shinned and grappled down the rope
And struggled to release it. But in vain.
'This man can't bear our life here and will drown,'

The abbot said, 'unless we help him.' So
They did, the freed ship sailed, and the man climbed
    back
Out of the marvellous as he had known it.

Seamus Heaney

Abou Ben Adhem

Abou Ben Adhem (may his tribe increase!)
Awoke one night from a deep dream of peace,
And saw, within the moonlight in his room,
Making it rich, and like a lily in bloom,
An angel writing in a book of gold:
Exceeding peace had made Ben Adhem bold,
And to the presence in the room he said,
'What writest thou?' The vision raised its head,
And with a look made of all sweet accord,
Answered, 'The names of those who love the Lord.'
'And is mine one?' said Abou. 'Nay, not so,'
Replied the angel. Abou spoke more low,
But cheerily still; and said, 'I pray thee, then,
Write me as one that loves his fellow men.'
The angel wrote, and vanished. The next night
It came again with a great wakening light,
And showed the names whom love of God had blest,
And lo! Ben Adhem's name led all the rest.

Leigh Hunt

Everyone sang

Everyone suddenly burst out singing;
And I was fill'd with such delight
As prison'd birds must find in freedom
Winging wildly across the white
Orchards and dark-green fields; on; on; and out of sight.

Everyone's voice was suddenly lifted,
And beauty came like the setting sun:
My heart was shaken with tears; and horror
Drifted away…O but Everyone
Was a bird; and the song was wordless; the singing will
    never be done.

Siegfried Sassoon

What are years

      What is our innocence,
what is our guilt? All are
      naked, none is safe. And whence
is courage; the unanswered question,
the resolute doubt –
dumbly calling, deafly listening – that
in misfortune, even death,
      encourages others
      and in its defeat, stirs

      the soul to be strong? He
sees deep and is glad, who
      accedes to mortality
and in his imprisonment rises
upon himself as
the sea in a chasm, struggling to be
free and unable to be,
      in its surrendering
      finds it continuing.

      So he who strongly feels
behaves. The very bird,
      grown taller as he sings, steels
his form straight up. Though he is captive,
his mighty singing
says, satisfaction is a lowly
thing, how pure a thing is joy.
            This is mortality,
            this is eternity.

Marianne Moore

Haiku

Skylark sings all
day, and day
not long enough.

Basho
(Translated from the Chinese by Lucien Stryk)

Midsummer, Tobago

Broad sun-stoned beaches.

White heat.
A green river.

A bridge,
scorched yellow palms

from the summer-sleeping house
drowsing through August.

Days I have held,
days I have lost,

days that outgrow, like daughters,
my harboring arms.

Derek Walcott

'Sleep wrapped you in green leaves'
from Mythistorema

Quid πλατανὼν opacissimuss?

Sleep wrapped you in green leaves like a tree
you breathed like a tree in the quiet light
in the limpid spring I looked at your face:
eyelids closed, eyelashes brushing the water.
In the soft grass my fingers found your fingers
I held your pulse a moment
and felt elsewhere your heart's pain.

Under the plane tree, near the water, among laurel
sleep moved you and scattered you
around me, near me, without my being able to touch the
     whole of you –
one as you were with your silence;
seeing your shadow grow and diminish,
lose itself in the other shadows, in the other
world that let you go yet held you back.

The life that they gave us to live, we lived.
Pity those who wait with such patience
lost in the black laurel under the heavy plane trees
and those, alone, who speak to cisterns and wells
and drown in the voice's circles.

Pity the companion who shared our privation and our
    sweat
and plunged into the sun like a crow beyond the ruins,
without hope of enjoying our reward.

Give us, outside sleep, serenity.

George Seferis
(Translated from the Greek by Edmund Keeley and Philip Sherrard)

Song, from The Princess

Now sleeps the crimson petal, now the white;
Nor waves the cypress in the palace walk;
Nor winks the gold fin in the porphyry font:
The fire-fly wakens: waken thou with me.

Now droops the milkwhite peacock like a ghost,
And like a ghost she glimmers on to me.

Now lies the Earth all Danaë to the stars,
And all thy heart lies open unto me.

Now slides the silent meteor on, and leaves
A shining furrow, as thy thoughts in me.

Now folds the lily all her sweetness up,
And slips into the bosom of the lake:
So fold thyself, my dearest, thou, and slip
Into my bosom and be lost in me.

Lord Alfred Tennyson

Do not stand at my grave and weep

Do not stand at my grave and weep;
I am not there. I do not sleep.
I am a thousand winds that blow.
I am the diamond glints on snow.
I am the sunlight on ripened grain.
I am the gentle autumn rain.
When you awaken in the morning's hush
I am the swift uplifting rush
Of quiet birds in circled flight.
I am the soft stars that shine at night.
Do not stand at my grave and cry;
I am not there. I did not die.

Anonymous

Let evening come

Let the light of late afternoon
shine through chinks in the barn, moving
up the bales as the sun moves down.

Let the cricket take up chafing
as a woman takes up her needles
and her yarn. Let evening come.

Let dew collect on the hoe abandoned
in long grass. Let the stars appear
and the moon disclose her silver horn.

Let the fox go back to its sandy den.
Let the wind die down. Let the shed
go black inside. Let evening come.

To the bottle in the ditch, to the scoop
in the oats, to air in the lung
let evening come.

Let it come, as it will, and don't
be afraid. God does not leave us
comfortless, so let evening come.

Jane Kenyon

Mother is dead

The branches' snow is like the cotton fluff
she wore in her aching ears. In this dead huff
after storm shall we speak of love?

As my absent father's distrait wife
she worked for us – knew us by sight.

We know her now by the way the snow
protects the plants before they go.

Lorine Niedecker

Stopping by woods on a snowy evening

Whose woods these are I think I know,
His house is in the village, though;
He will not see me stopping here
To watch his woods fill up with snow.

My little horse must think it queer
To stop without a farmhouse near
Between the woods and frozen lake
The darkest evening of the year.

He gives his harness bells a shake
To ask if there is some mistake.
The only other sound's the sweep
Of easy wind and downy flake.

The woods are lovely, dark, and deep,
But I have promises to keep,
And miles to go before I sleep,
And miles to go before I sleep.

Robert Frost

'She tells her love while half asleep'

She tells her love while half asleep
    In the dark hours,
        with half-words whispered low:
As Earth stirs in her winter sleep
    And puts out grass and flowers
        Despite the snow,
        Despite the falling snow.

Robert Graves

Let it be forgotten

Let it be forgotten, as a flower is forgotten,
    Forgotten as a fire that once was singing gold,
Let it be forgotten for ever and ever,
    Time is a kind friend, he will make us old.

If anyone asks, say it was forgotten
    Long and long ago,
As a flower, as a fire, as a hushed footfall
    In a long forgotten snow.

Sara Teasdale

A quiet joy

I'm standing in a place where I once loved.
The rain is falling. The rain is my home.

I think words of longing: a landscape
out to the very edge of what's possible.

I remember you waving your hand
as if wiping mist from the windowpane,

and your face, as if enlarged
from an old blurred photo.

Once I committed a terrible wrong
to myself and others.

But the world is beautifully made for doing good
and for resting, like a park bench

And late in life I discovered
a quiet joy
like a serious disease that's discovered too late:

just a little time left now for quiet joy.

Yehuda Amichai
(*Translated from the Hebrew by Chana Bloch*)

Bus stop

Lights are burning
In quiet rooms
Where lives go on
Resembling ours.

The quiet lives
That follow us –
These lives we lead
But do not own –

Stand in the rain
So quietly
When we are gone,
So quietly…

And the last bus
Comes letting dark
Umbrellas out –
Black flowers, black flowers.

And lives go on.
And lives go on
Like sudden lights
At street corners

Or like the lights
In quiet rooms
Left on for hours,
Burning, burning.

Donald Justice

Santuario at Chimayo

It's so quiet among the carved saints,
the votives giving out, one by one, the old
woman scraping wax and bent wicks.

Grief lights them again. Photographs
of the dead are tucked into the corners
of framed Christs, dogtags slung

from a punched-tin cross – *Jaime Escalero*,
his number and blood type.
And *Catholic*. Even the tourists are hushed

by so much evidence of faith.
In the room behind the altar
a small hole holds the dirt

said to heal. The blind
come here, and the broken-hearted.
They squat down

to take the earth
in their hands and let it run through.
Every afternoon

the old woman slips new candles
into their sheaths
and the random light from cameras

is like souls entering
or abandoning the world,
each with that same brightness.

Kim Addonizio

Sonnet XXII from the Portuguese

When our two souls stand up erect and strong,
Face to face, silent, drawing nigh and nigher,
Until the lengthening wings break into fire
At either curvéd point, – what bitter wrong
Can the earth do to us, that we should not long
Be here contented? Think. In mounting higher,
The angels would press on us, and aspire
To drop some golden orb of perfect song
Into our deep, dear silence. Let us stay
Rather on earth, Belovèd, – where the unfit
Contrarious moods of men recoil away
And isolate pure spirits, and permit
A place to stand and love in for a day,
With darkness and the death-hour rounding it.

Elizabeth Barrett Browning

Never enough of living

Never, my heart, is there enough of living,
since only in thee is loveliness so sweet pain;
Only for thee the willows will be giving
Their quiet fringes to the dreaming river;
Only for thee so the light grasses ever
Are hollowed by the print of windy feet,
And breathe hill weather on the misty plain;
And were no rapture of them in thy beat,
For every hour of sky
Stillborn in gladness would the waters wear
Colors of air translucently,
And the stars sleep there.

Gently, my heart, nor let one moment ever
Be spilled from the brief fulness of thine urn.
Plunge in its exultation star and star,
Sea and plumed sea in turn.
O still, my heart, nor spill this moment ever.

Leonie Adams

This moment

This Moment

A neighborhood.
At dusk.

Things are getting ready
to happen
out of sight.

Stars and moths.
And rinds slanting around fruit.

But not yet.

One tree is black.
One window is yellow as butter.

A woman leans down to catch a child
who has run into her arms
this moment.

Stars rise.
Moths flutter.
Apples sweeten in the dark.

Eavan Boland

The wild geese

horseback on Sunday morning,
harvest over, we taste persimmon
and wild grape, sharp sweet
of summer's end. In time's maze
over the fall fields, we name names
that went west from here, names
that rest on graves. We open
a persimmon seed to find the tree
that stands in promise,
pale, in the seed's marrow.
Geese appear high over us,
pass, and the sky closes. Abandon,
as in love or sleep, holds
them to their way, clear
in the ancient faith: what we need
is here. And we pray, not
for new earth or heaven, but to be
quiet in heart, and in eye,
clear. What we need is here.

Wendell Berry

Broceliande

for Marie-Geneviève Havel

Yes, there is a vault in the ruined castle.
Yes, there is a woman waking beside the
gleaming sword she drew from the stone of childhood:
hers, if she bore it.

She has found her way through the singing forest.
She has gotten lost in the maze of cobbled
streets in ancient towns, where no lovely stranger
spoke the right language.

Sometimes she inhabits the spiring cities
architects project out of science fiction
dreams, but she illuminates them with different
voyages, visions:

with tomato plants, with the cat who answers
when he's called, with music-hall lyrics, work-scarred
hands on a steering-wheel, the jeweled secret
name of a lover.

Here, the water plunges beneath the cliff face.
Here, the locomotive purrs in the station.
Here, beneath viridian skies, a window
glistens at midnight.

Marilyn Hacker

the mississippi river empties into the gulf

and the gulf enters the sea and so forth,
none of them emptying anything,
all of them carrying yesterday
forever on their white tipped backs,
all of them dragging forward tomorrow.
it is the great circulation
of the earth's body, like the blood
of the gods, this river in which the past
is always flowing. every water
is the same water coming round.
everyday someone is standing on the edge
of this river, staring into time,
whispering mistakenly:
only here. only now.

Lucille Clifton

The Negro speaks of rivers

I've known rivers:
I've known rivers ancient as the world and older than
    the flow of human blood in human veins.

My soul has grown deep like the rivers.

I bathed in the Euphrates when dawns were young.
I built my hut near the Congo and it lulled me to sleep.

I looked upon the Nile and raised the pyramids above it.
I heard the singing of the Mississippi when Abe Lincoln
    went down to New Orleans, and I've seen its muddy
    bosom turn all golden in the sunset.

I've known rivers:
Ancient, dusky rivers.

My soul has grown deep like the rivers.

Langston Hughes

Oh, earth, wait for me

Return me, oh sun,
to my country destiny,
rain of the ancient woods.
Bring me back its aroma, and the swords
falling from the sky,
the solitary peace of pasture and rock,
the damp at the river margins,
the smell of the larch tree,
the wind alive like a heart
beating in the crowded remoteness
of the towering araucaria.

Earth, give me back your pristine gifts,
towers of silence which rose from
the solemnity of their roots.
I want to go back to being what I haven't been,
to learn to return from such depths
that among all natural things
I may live or not live. I don't mind
being one stone more, the dark stone,
the pure stone that the river bears away.

Pablo Neruda
(Translated from the Spanish by Alastair Reid)

Dover beach

The sea is calm tonight.
The tide is full, the moon lies fair
Upon the straits; – on the French coast the light
Gleams and is gone; the cliffs of England stand,
Glimmering and vast, out in the tranquil bay.
Come to the window, sweet is the night air!
Only, from the long line of spray
Where the sea meets the moon-blanch'd land,
Listen! you hear the grating roar
Of pebbles which the waves draw back, and fling,
At their return, up the high strand,
Begin, and cease, and then again begin,
With tremulous cadence slow, and bring
The eternal note of sadness in.

Sophocles long ago
Heard it on the Aegean, and it brought
Into his mind the turbid ebb and flow
Of human misery; we
Find also in the sound a thought,
Hearing it by this distant northern sea.

The Sea of Faith
Was once, too, at the full, and round earth's shore
Lay like the folds of a bright girdle furl'd.

But now I only hear
Its melancholy, long, withdrawing roar,
Retreating, to the breath
Of the night-wind, down the vast edges drear
And naked shingles of the world.

Ah, love, let us be true
to one another! for the world, which seems
to lie before us like a land of dreams,
So various, so beautiful, so new,
Hath really neither joy, nor love, nor light,
Nor certitude, nor peace, nor help for pain;
And we are here as on a darkling plain
Swept with confused alarms of struggle and flight,
where ignorant armies clash by night.

Matthew Arnold

Poem

You who wear shirts
ripped at the collars:

>   it has come:
>   the great calm
>   with its harvest of silence:

>   all lips have been sewn,
>   perhaps some wounds also.

And rebels,
my friends:

>   fill your vases with water
>   for spring is here:

>   in this blossoming
>   of wounds,

>   some roses may also.

Faiz Ahmed Faiz
(Translated from the Urdu by Agha Shahid Ali)

A game of chess

to John Brodie

Nightfall: the town's chromatic nocturne wakes
dark brilliance on the river; colours drift
and tremble as enormous shadows lift
Orion to his place. The heart remakes
that peace torn in the blaze of day. Inside
your room are music, warmth and wine, the board
with chessmen set for play. The harpsichord
begins a fugue; delight is multiplied.

A game: the heart's impossible ideal –
to choose among a host of paths, and know
that if the kingdom crumbles one can yield
and have the choice again. Abstract and real
joined in their trance of thought, two players show
the calm of gods above a troubled field.

Gwen Harwood

from The Ruba'iyat

'Tis all a Chequer-board of Nights and Days
Where Destiny with Men for Pieces plays:
    Hither and thither moves, and mates, and slays,
And one by one back in the Closet lays.

Omar Khayam
(Translated from the Persian by Edward Fitzgerald)

Brahma

If the red slayer think he slays
    Or if the slain think he is slain,
They know not well the subtle ways
    I keep, and pass, and turn again.

Far or forgot to me is near;
    Shadow and sunlight are the same;
The vanished gods to me appear;
    And one to me are shame and fame.

They reckon ill who leave me out;
    When me they fly, I am the wings;
I am the doubter and the doubt,
    And I the hymn the Brahmin sings.

The strong gods pine for my abode,
    And pine in vain the sacred Seven;
But thou, meek lover of the good!
    Find me, and turn thy back on heaven.

Ralph Waldo Emerson

The new Colossus

Not like the brazen giant of Greek fame,
With conquering limbs astride from land to land;
Here at our sea-washed, sunset gates shall stand
A mighty woman with a torch, whose flame
Is the imprisoned lightning, and her name
Mother of Exiles. From her beacon-hand
Glows world-wide welcome; her mild eyes command
The air-bridged harbor that twin cities frame.
'Keep, ancient lands, your storied pomp!' cries she
With silent lips. 'Give me your tired, your poor,
Your huddled masses yearning to breathe free,
The wretched refuse of your teeming shore.
Send these, the homeless, tempest-tost to me,
I lift my lamp beside the golden door!'

Emma Lazarus

Good girl

Hold up the universe, good girl. Hold up
the tent that is the sky of your world at which
you are the narrow center pole, good girl. Rup-
ture is the enemy. Keep all whole. The itch
to be yourself, plump and bending, below a sky
unending, held up by God forever
is denied by you as Central Control. Sever
yourself, poor false Atlas, poor "Atlesse," lie
recumbent below the sky. Nothing falls down,
except you, luscious and limited on the ground.
Holding everything up, always on your own,
creates a loneliness so profound
you are nothing but a column, good girl,
a temple ruin against a sky held up
by forces beyond you. Let yourself curl
up: a fleshy foetal figure cupped
about its own vibrant soul. You are
the universe about its pole. God's not far.

Molly Peacock

From the Persian

Naked out of the dark we came.
Naked into the dark we go.
Come to my arms, naked in the dark.

Anonymous
(Translated from the Persian by Kenneth Rexroth)

Index of first lines

Biographical notes

Compiled by the publishers

Leonie Adams (1899–1988): Born in New York City. Educator, consultant, editor, and poet, she worked at The Metropolitan Museum of Art and lectured at New Jersey College for Women.

Kim Addonizio (1954–): Born in Washington D.C. and author of three books of poetry. Her latest collection, *What Is This Thing Called Love* was published in 2004. Addonizio currently teaches private poetry workshops in Oakland, California.

Yehuda Amichai (1924–2000): Born in Germany, emigrated to Palestine in 1936. World-famous contemporary Hebrew poet. His collections in English include *Open Closed Open* (2000) and *Selected Poetry* (1996).

Matthew Arnold (1822–1888): Great Victorian poet and critic, he was Inspector of Schools for 35 years, later Professor of Poetry at Oxford.

John Ashbery (1927–): Winner of the Pulitzer Prize, the National Book Critics Circle Award, and the National Book Award. His recent collection *Chinese Whispers* was published in 2003.

W. H. Auden (1907–1973): One of the most influential poets of the 20th century, he was born in England, but became an American citizen in 1946. His *Collected Poems* was published in 1991.

Basho (1644–1694): Born in Ueno, Japan. Master of the Haiku form, refining elements of Buddhist and Taoist symbolism.

Charles Baudelaire (1821–1867): Born in Paris. The most famous (and influential) French poet of the 19th century, he is world-renowned for his ground-breaking collection, *Les Fleurs du Mal*.

Wendell Berry (1934–): Born in Kentucky. Author of more than 30 books of poetry, essays, and novels. *The Collected Poems of Wendell Berry* was published in 1987.

Laurence Binyon (1869–1943): Born in Lancaster, England. Poet and art critic, he won the Newdigate Poetry Prize at Oxford. His most famous poems reflect his experiences in the First World War.

Elizabeth Bishop (1911–1979): Born in Massachusetts, she grew up in Canada, and lived much of her life in Brazil. She won every major US poetry award including the Pulitzer Prize for Poetry and the National Book Award. Her *Complete Poems* was published in 1983.

William Blake (1757–1827): Author of *Songs of Innocence* and *Songs of Experience*. Poet and engraver, now world-famous for his visionary works, Blake's genius was not widely recognized in his day.

Eavan Boland (1944–): Born in Ireland. Boland is Professor of English at Stanford University. Her recent collections include *Against Love Poetry* (2001), *The Lost Land* (1998), and *In a Time of Violence* (1994).

Robert Browning (1812–1889): Born in London. Renowned for his development of the dramatic monologue, Browning became one of the foremost Victorian poets. He eloped to Italy with the poet Elizabeth Barrett in 1846.

Elizabeth Barrett Browning (1806–1861): Famous for her widely anthologized *Sonnets from the Portuguese*, she was a prolific poet and translator. She married her fellow poet, Robert Browning.

Hayden Carruth (1921–): Born in Connecticut, he lived for many years in Vermont and now lives in upstate New York. He is also known for his essays on contemporary poetry and on jazz. Carruth received the National Book Award for Poetry for *Scrambled Eggs and Whiskey* in 1996. His most recent collection is *Doctor Jazz* (2002).

John Clare (1793–1864): Born in Helpston, Northamptonshire, he was known as the "peasant poet." After early literary success, interest in his later work faded rapidly. He spent the second half of his life in a mental asylum. An edition of his *Selected Poems* was published in 2000.

Lucille Clifton (1936–): Born in Depew, New York. She won the National Book Award in 2001 for *Blessing the Boats: New and Selected Poems*. Other titles include *The Terrible Stories* (1995), which was nominated for the National Book Award, and *The Book of Light* (1993).

Samuel Taylor Coleridge (1772–1834): Born in Devonshire. Along with William Wordsworth, he was a leader of the British Romantic movement. In 1798 the two men collaborated on *Lyrical Ballads*, one of the first great works of the Romantic school of poetry.

Lorna Crozier (1948–): A Canadian poet who teaches creative writing at the University of Victoria. Her recent collections include *A Saving Grace: The Collected Poems of Mrs. Bentley*, (1996), *What the Living Won't Let Go*, (1999)*, and *Apocrypha of Light* (2000).

Emily Dickinson (1830–1886): A giant presence in 19th-century American poetry, she lived as a virtual recluse at her home in Amherst, Massachusetts. Only seven of her poems were published in her lifetime—her work was collected and published after her death.

Jane Duran (1944–): Born in Cuba and brought up in the USA and Chile. She has lived in London since 1966. Her book, *Breathe Now, Breathe*, won the 1995 Forward Prize for the Best First Collection, and her *Silences from the Spanish Civil War* was published in 2002.

T. S. Eliot (1888–1965): Born in St. Louis, Missouri. Renowned for *The Waste Land* and *The Four Quartets*, he won the Nobel Prize for Poetry in 1948. Perhaps the most influential poet and critic of the 20th century.

Ralph Waldo Emerson (1803–1882): Born in Boston, Massachusetts, he was an acclaimed poet, essayist, and philosopher. He became the chief spokesman for Transcendentalism, a literary and philosophical movement that spoke against scientific rationalism.

Faiz Ahmed Faiz (1911–1984): Born and educated in Pakistan, Faiz was the first Asian poet to be awarded the Lenin Peace Prize in 1963. He was also nominated for the Nobel Prize.

Robert Frost (1874–1963): Born in California, he spent most of his life in New England. Frost won the Pulitzer Prize for poetry four times. His poetry collections include *New Hampshire* (1923), *From Snow to Snow* (1936), *A Witness Tree* (1942), *Come In, and Other Poems* (1943), *Masque of Reason* (1945), *Steeple Bush* (1947), and *In the Clearing* (1962).

Tess Gallagher (1943–): Born in Port Angeles, Washington. An award-winning poet, essayist, novelist, and playwright. Her recent collections include *My Black Horse: New and Selected Poems* (1995), *Owl-Spirit Dwelling* (1994), and *Moon Crossing Bridge* (1992).

Louise Glück (1943–): Born in New York City. She is the author of seven books of poetry, including *The Seven Ages* (2001), *Meadowlands* (1996), *The Wild Iris* (1992), which received the Pulitzer Prize, and

The Triumph of Achilles (1985), which received the National Book Critics Circle Award. She was Poet Laureate of the United States in 2003–2004.

W. S. Graham (1918–1986): Born in Greenock, Scotland. He was published by T. S. Eliot at Faber Books. His collections include *Malcolm Mooney's Land* (1970) and *Implements in Their Places* (1977). His *New Collected Poems* was published in 2004.

Robert Graves (1895–1985): British poet, novelist, essayist, he survived the Battle of the Somme in 1916, and eventually left England to live in Mallorca. His book, *The White Goddess,* influenced generations of writers.

Marilyn Hacker (1942–): Born in New York City. She was editor of *The Kenyon Review* from 1990 to 1994, and has received numerous honors, including the National Book Award. She lives in New York City and Paris. Her most recent collection, *Desesperanto*, was published in 2003.

Donald Hall (1928–): Born in New Haven, Connecticut. Hall served as poetry editor for *Paris Review.* Author of 15 books of poetry, and winner of many awards, he has taught at Stanford, Harvard, and the University of Michigan. He was married to fellow poet, the late Jane Kenyon. His latest book of poems is *The Painted Bed* (2002).

Thomas Hardy (1840–1928): Though better known for his novels, he dedicated the last 30 years of his life to poetry. His books include *Wessex Poems* (1898), *Time's Laughingstocks* (1909), *Satires of Circumstance* (1914), and *Moments of Vision* (1917). A recent edition of *Thomas Hardy: The Complete Poems* was published in 2002.

Gwen Harwood (1920–1995): A distinguished Australian poet, she won the Patrick White Award in 1978, and the Victoria Premier's Literary Award for Poetry in 1989. Her *Collected Poems* was published in 2003.

Lee Harwood (1939–): British poet who studied English at Queen Mary College, University of London. His latest book, *Collected Poems*, was published in 2004.

Seamus Heaney (1939–): Born In Castledawson, Northern Ireland. He won the Nobel Prize for Poetry in 1995, and the Whitbread Book of the Year Award for his translation of Beowulf. He has taught at Berkeley, Harvard, and Oxford. Author of 13 poetry collections, his latest book is *Electric Light*, published 2001.

George Herbert (1593–1633): Eminent poet-priest, born in Wales. Educated at Trinity College Cambridge, he was a member of Parliament, and was canon of Lincoln Cathedral. He wrote in English and Latin.

Jane Hirshfield (1953–): Born in New York City. Her collection, *Given Sugar, Given Salt,* was finalist for the 2001 National Book Critics Circle Award, and winner of the Bay Area Book Reviewers Award. She teaches Bennington College's MFA Writing Seminars.

Kakinomoto no Hitomaro (*c.* 660–708) Early Japanese lyric poet. He is considered to be the greatest poet in the *Manyôshu*, the oldest Japanese poetry anthology in existence.

A. D. Hope (1907–2000): Born in Cooma, Australia, he is highly regarded for his elegies and satires. His *Selected Poems* was published in 1985.

Gerard Manley Hopkins (1844–1889): Born in Stratford, London. A Jesuit priest and poet, little of his poetry was published during his lifetime. He is now regarded as a major British poet.

Langston Hughes (1902–1967): Born in Joplin, Missouri. Poet, essayist, and writer of autobiography, fiction, and drama, Hughes was a prominent figure of the Harlem Renaissance. He published ten books of poetry, including *Montage of a Dream Deferred*.

Ted Hughes (1930–1998): Born in Yorkshire. His best-known works include *The Hawk in the Rain* (1957), *Crow* (1970), and his late *Birthday Letters* (1998) based on his marriage to fellow poet Sylvia Plath. He was Poet Laureate of England for the last 13 years of his life.

Leigh Hunt (1784–1859): Born in Southgate, Middlesex. Hunt was a prolific poet, as well as a journalist, a dramatic, and a literary critic. He was one of the first to recognize the genius of Shelley and Keats.

Elizabeth Jennings (1926–2001): A renowned English poet, born in Lincolnshire, she studied at St. Anne's College, Oxford. Her *Collected Poems* was published in 1987.

Donald Justice (1925–2004): Born in Miami, Florida. He won the Pulitzer Prize for poetry in 1980, and the Bollingen Prize in 1991. His *New and Selected Poems* was published in 1995 and *Orpheus Hesitated Beside the Black River* was published in 2004.

Patrick Kavanagh (1904–1967): Born in County Monaghan, Ireland, he struggled to live as a farmer for the first half of his life. He became active in the literary scene of Dublin in the 1930s, writing features and reviews. His best-known poem, *The Great Hunger* (1942), describes the Irish farmer's daily poverty and inhibitions.

John Keats (1795–1821): Born in London. A much loved Romantic poet, Keats died when he was 25, and had published only 54 poems. The renowned author of *Hyperion* and *Endymion*, he is particularly admired for his sonnets and odes.

Jane Kenyon (1947–1995): Appointed New Hampshire's Poet Laureate in 1995. She published four collections: *Constance* (1993), *Let Evening Come* (1990), *The Boat of Quiet Hours* (1986), and *From Room to Room* (1978).

Kesa'i: Medieval Persian poet.

Omar Khayam (1044–1123): Born in Nishapur, Iran. One of the most widely known Persian poets, Khayam's work *The Rubaiyat* was translated by Edward Fitzgerald, the English poet and translator.

Galway Kinnell (1927–): Born in Rhode Island. He was awarded both the Pulitzer Prize for Poetry and the National Book Award for Poetry for his *Selected Poems* (1980). He is a visiting professor at New York University, but lives mostly in Vermont.

Philip Larkin (1922–1985): Born in Coventry. While writing collections of poetry such as *The Whitsun Weddings* and *High Windows* that made him one of the pre-eminent poets of his generation, he worked as a librarian in the provincial city of Hull.

Dorianne Laux (1952–): Born in Augusta, Maine. Associate Professor at the University of Oregon's Program in Creative Writing, Laux is the author of three poetry collections—*Smoke* (2000), *What We Carry* (1994), and *Awake* (1990).

D. H. Lawrence (1885–1930): Born in Eastwood, Nottinghamshire. Though better known as a novelist, Lawrence published nine poetry collections. His *Collected Poems* was published in 1964.

Emma Lazarus (1849–1887): She grew up in New York and Newport, Rhode Island, and was mentored by poet Ralph Waldo Emerson.

Giacomo Leopardi (1798–1837): Born in Recanati, Italy. Widely admired and considered by some to be second only to the Italian poet Petrarch in poetic genius.

Michael Longley (1939–): Born in Belfast, Northern Ireland. Longley worked as a schoolteacher until he joined the Arts Council of Northern Ireland in 1970. His collection, *The Weather in Japan* (2000), won the Hawthornden Prize, the T. S. Eliot Prize, and the Irish Times Prize for Poetry. His latest title *Snow Water* was published in 2004.

Norman MacCaig (1910–1996): Born in Edinburgh, Scotland. MacCaig published 14 collections of poetry. He was appointed Fellow in Creative Writing at Edinburgh in 1967, and in 1970 became a reader in poetry at the University of Stirling.

Louis MacNeice (1907–1963): Born in Belfast, Northern Ireland. The Irish landscape of his childhood is a prominent aspect of his work. Educated at Oxford, he taught Greek before working as a scriptwriter and producer for the BBC. His *Autumn Journal,* published in 1938, chronicles the arrival of World War II in England.

Derek Mahon (1941–): Born in Belfast, Northern Ireland. A highly acclaimed poet, he has published over 18 poetry collections. They include *The Hudson Letter* (1996), *Selected Poems* (1993), *The Yaddo Letter* (1992), *Antarctica* (1985), and *The Hunt by Night* (1982).

Andrew Marvell (1621–1678): Born In Yorkshire. Educated at Trinity College, Cambridge, he was known primarily as a satirist during his lifetime. Marvell's reputation as a great poet came only after his death —his poems were published posthumously.

Charlotte Mew (1869–1928): Born in London, she lived for a while in Paris. Her poetry was greatly admired by writers such as Thomas Hardy, Siegfried Sassoon, and Ezra Pound.

Marianne Moore (1887–1972): Born near St. Louis, Missouri. She edited the influential modernist magazine *Dial* from 1925 to 1929. Her poetry was highly acclaimed, winning her the Bollingen Prize, the National Book Award for Poetry, and the Pulitzer Prize for Poetry.

Marilyn Nelson (1946–): Born in Ohio. Professor of English at the University of Connecticut, Nelson is a widely acclaimed poet. One of her collections, *The Fields of Praise: New and Selected Poems*, was nominated for three separate awards, including the 1997 National Book Award.

Pablo Neruda (1904–1973): Internationally acclaimed as the greatest Latin-American poet since Darío, he was awarded the International Peace Prize in 1950, the Lenin Peace Prize in 1953, and the Nobel Prize for Literature in 1971.

Lorine Niedecker (1970–1903): Born in Wisconsin. Her poems did not receive wide critical attention until late in her life. Since her death, three volumes of her poetry have been published, including *The Selected Poems of Lorine Niedecker* published in 1985, and her *Collected Works*, which appeared in 2002.

Naomi Shihab Nye (1952–): A Palestinian-American born in St. Louis, Missouri, she currently lives and works in San Antonio, Texas. She is the author of several books of poems, including *19 Varieties of Gazelle: Poems of the Middle East* (2002), *Fuel* (1998), *Red Suitcase* (1994), and *Hugging the Jukebox* (1982).

Mary Oliver (1935–): Born in Ohio, she now lives in Provincetown, MA. She is the author of many volumes of poetry, including: *Why I Wake Early* (2004), *Owls and Other Fantasies: Poems and Essays* (2003), *Winter Hours: Prose, Prose Poems, and Poems* (1999), *White Pine* (1994), *New and Selected Poems* (1992), which won the National Book award, and *American Primitive* (1983), for which she won the Pulitzer Prize.

Molly Peacock (1947–): President Emerita of the Poetry Society of America, she instigated the Poetry in Motion program, which displays poetry on public transport. Her collections of poetry include *Cornucopia* (2002), *Original Love* (1995), *Take Heart* (1989), *Raw Heaven* (1984), and *And Live Apart* (1980).

Sylvia Plath (1932–1963): Born in Boston, Massachusetts and educated at Smith College and Newnham College, Cambridge. In England, Plath met and married the poet Ted Hughes. She published four collections of poetry, *The Colossus and Other Poems*, *Ariel*, *Crossing the Water*, and *Winter Trees*.

Li Po (701–762): Chinese poet of the Tang dynasty. Approximately 1,100 of his poems remain today. The poet Ezra Pound introduced his work to the West.

Marie Ponsot (1921–): Born in New York City. She received the National Book Critics Circle Award for *The Bird Catcher* in 1998. *Springing*, her selected poems, was published in 2002.

Rainer Maria Rilke (1875–1926): Born in Prague in 1895, he traveled widely. His last two books *Duino Elegies* and the *Sonnets to Orpheus* were written in Switzerland. *Rainer Maria Rilke: Selected Poems* (reissued in 1989) is a good introduction to his work.

Christina Rossetti (1830–1894): Born in London. Sister of the poet and Pre-Raphaelite painter, Dante Gabriel Rossetti, she is best known for *Goblin Market, and Other Poems* (1862).

Dante Gabriel Rossetti (1828–1882): Born in London, and a leading member of the Pre-Raphaelite Brotherhood, his twin passions were poetry and painting.

Siegfried Sassoon (1886–1967): Born in Kent. He fought in the First World War, and met fellow poets Robert Graves and Wilfred Owen who shared his horror of the experience. His *Collected Poems* was published in 1961.

George Seferis (1900–1971): Born in Smyrna. He was awarded the Nobel Prize in Literature in 1963. His *Collected Poems* was published in 1993.

William Shakespeare (1564–1616): Born in Stratford-on-Avon. Perhaps the greatest writer in the English language; he acted, lived, and wrote in London, but retired to his birthplace, Stratford-on-Avon.

Wallace Stevens (1879–1955): Born in Pennsylvania. He worked in various law firms while writing poetry. Author of a dozen volumes of verse, Stevens is ranked as a major American poet of the 20th century.

May Swenson (1913–1989): Born in Utah. Her poetry is prized for its fine observations of the natural world. She was Chancellor of The Academy of American Poets from 1980 to 1989. Her more recent work appeared in the collections *The Love Poems of May Swenson* (1991), *Nature: Poems Old and New* (1994), and *May Out West* (1996).

Sara Teasdale (1884–1933): Born in St. Louis, Missouri. Her many awards included the Columbia University Poetry Society Prize (which became the Pulitzer Prize for Poetry,) and the Poetry Society of America Prize.

Lord Alfred Tennyson (1809–1892): Born in Somersby, Lincolnshire. The publication of *In Memoriam* in 1850 made him one of Britain's most popular poets.

R. S. Thomas (1913–2000): Welsh poet, born in Cardiff, he was ordained in the Anglican Church in Wales, and served in various Welsh parishes. In 1964 he won the Queen's Gold Medal for Poetry, and was nominated for the 1996 Nobel Prize in Literature. *Collected Poems, 1945–1990* was published in 1990 and *R. S. Thomas: Poems 1960-1999* in 2000.

Chase Twichell (1950–): Born in New Haven, Connecticut. Winner of fellowships from both the Guggenheim Foundation and the National Endowment for the Arts. Her collection *The Snow Watcher* won the Alice Fay Di Castagnola Award from the Poetry Society of America in 1998.

Henry Vaughan (1622–1695): Born in Wales, and educated at Jesus College, Oxford. His work is considered to be among the finest religious poetry in English.

Virgil (70 B.C.–19 B.C.): A world-famous Roman poet, Virgil is renowned for his epic poems *The Georgics,* and *The Aeneid.*

Ellen Bryant Voigt (1943–): Born in Virginia. She was elected Chancellor of The Academy of American Poets in 2003, and is currently Vermont State Poet. Her collection *Shadow of Heaven* was a finalist for the 2002 National Book Award for Poetry

Diane Wakoski (1937–): Born in California. She has published more than 40 collections of poems, including *Argonaut Rose* (1998), *The Emerald City of Las Vegas* (1995), *Jason the Sailor* (1993), *Medea the Sorceress* (1991), and *Emerald Ice: Selected Poems 1962-1987* (1988), which won the Poetry Society of America's William Carlos Williams Award.

Derek Walcott (1930–): Saint Lucian poet and playwright who won the Nobel Prize for Literature in 1992. he has written eight collections of poetry—most recently *Tiepolo's Hound* (2000), *The Bounty* (1997), *Omeros* (1990), and *The Arkansas Testament* (1987).

Jayne O. Wayne: (1938–): American poet living in St. Louis, Missouri. Her book *Strange Heart* (1996) was selected by James Tate for the 1995 Marianne Moore Poetry Prize, and also received the 1996 Society of Midland Authors Poetry Award.

Wang Wei (699–761): Chinese poet, painter and civil servant, he wrote in the formal tradition of "poetry of retreat."

Walt Whitman (1819–1892): Born in Long Island, New York. A poet, essayist, and journalist, Whitman is a giant presence in American literature. He is best known for the poems in *Leaves of Grass* and *Drum Taps*. He served as a hospital nurse during the American Civil War, an experience that greatly affected him.

William Carlos Williams (1883–1963): Born in New Jersey. One of America's best known poets, and winner of the National Book Award and the Pulitzer Prize, Williams was both a dedicated poet and a full time physician. His poetry collections include *Journey to Love* and *The Broken Span*.

William Wordsworth (1770–1850): Born in Cumbria, Northumberland. His preface to his *Lyrical Ballads* was a radical literary statement, and established the importance of using common language in poetry.

James Wright (1927–1980): Born in Ohio. A highly esteemed American poet who won the Pulitzer Prize for Literature in 1966, he taught at the University of Minnesota and Hunter College, New York.

Elinor Wylie (1885–1928): Born in New Jersey. She was the author of four books of poems and four novels.

W. B. Yeats (1865–1939): Born in Dublin, he is regarded as one of the greatest of all Irish poets. Yeats received the Nobel Prize for Literature in 1923. His major collections include *The Wind Among the Reeds* (1899), *Responsibilities and Other Poems* (1916), *The Wild Swans at Coole* (1919), and *The Tower* (1929).

Sources & Acknowledgements

Leonie Adams: 'Never Enough of Living' from *Poems: A Selection* (Funk & Wagnall, 1954); Kim Addonizio: 'Santuario at Chimayo' from *In Sublette's Barn* (Fall, 1998), © Kim Addonizio, by permission of the author; Yehuda Amichai: 'A Quiet Joy' from *Selected Poems* translated by Chana Bloch (Faber & Faber, 2000); Anonymous: 'From the Persian' translated by Kenneth Rexroth (Copper Canyon Press, 1997); John Ashbery: 'What is Poetry?' from *Houseboat Days* (The Viking Press/Penguin Books, 1977); W. H. Auden: 'The More Loving One' from *Collected Shorter Poems 1927–1957* (Faber & Faber, 1996), © W. H. Auden, 1966; Basho: from *On Love and Barley, Haiku of Basho* translated by Lucien Stryk (Penguin Classics, 1985); Charles Baudelaire: 'The Giantess' from *French Love Poems* translated by Alistair Elliot (Bloodaxe Books, 1991), by permission of the publisher; Wendell Berry: 'Wild Geese' from T*he Country of Marriage* (Harcourt Brace Jovanovich, 1973); Laurence Binyon: 'Winter Sunrise' from *Collected Poems of Laurence Binyon* (Macmillan, 1931), by permission of The Society of Authors as the Literary Representative of the Estate of Laurence Binyon; Elizabeth Bishop: 'Sleeping on the Ceiling' from *The Complete Poems 1927–1979* (The Hogarth Press, 1984), © 1979, 1983 by Alice Helen Methfessel; Eavan Boland: 'Writing in a Time of Violence' from *Collected Poems* (Carcanet Press, 1995), by permission of the publisher; Hayden Carruth: 'Sonnet' from *Collected Shorter Poems 1946–1991* (Copper Canyon Press, 1991); Lucille Clifton: 'the mississippi river empties into the gulf' from *The Terrible Stories* (BOA Editions, 1996); Lorna Crozier: 'Calm' from *Poetry International, 7/8* (2003–4); Emily Dickinson: 'I Dwell in Possibility' from *The Poems of Emily Dickinson,* edited by Thomas H. Johnson (Cambridge, Massachusetts: The Belknap Press of Harvard University Press), © 1951, 1955, 1979 by the President and Fellows of Harvard College; Jane Duran: 'Lullaby' by permission of the author; T. S. Eliot: 'Usk' from *Collected Poems 1909–1962* (Faber & Faber, 1974); Faiz Ahmed Faiz: 'Poem' translated by Agha Shahid Ali, from *The Rebel's Silhouette, Selected Poems* (University of Massachusetts Press, 1995); Robert Frost: 'Stopping by Woods on a Snowy Evening' from *Selected Poems* (Penguin Poets, 1955), by permission of the Estate of Robert Frost and The Random House Group Ltd; Tess Gallagher: 'Blue Grapes' from *Moon Crossing Bridge* (Graywolf Press, 1992); Louise Gluck: 'Lullaby', from *The Wild Iris* (Carcanet Press, 1992), by permission of the publisher; W. S. Graham: 'I Leave This At Your Ear' from *Selected Poems* (Faber & Faber, 1996), © The Estate of W. S. Graham, by permission of Margaret Snow, Literary Executor for the Estate of W. S. Graham; Robert Graves: 'She Tells Her Love While Half Asleep', from *Complete Poems* (Carcanet Press, 2000), by permission of the publisher; Marilyn Hacker: 'Broceliande' from *Squares and Courtyards* (W.W. Norton, 2000), © 2000 by Marilyn Hacker; Donald Hall: 'Christmas Party at the South Danbury Church' from *New Criterion* (January, 1995); Gwen Harwood: 'A Game of Chess' from *Collected Poems* (Oxford University Press, 1991), © Gwen Harwood, 1975,

1985, 1990, 1991; Lee Harwood: 'Gorgeous – yet another Brighton poem' from
Collected Poems (Shearsman Books, 2004), by permission of the author; Seamus
Heaney: from 'Lightenings. Viii' in *Seeing Things* (Faber & Faber, 1991); Jane
Hirshfield: 'Lying' from *Lives of the Heart* (Harper/Perennial Books, 1997);
Kakinomoto No Hitomaro: 'When I Gathered Flowers' translated by Kenneth
Rexroth, from *One Hundred Poems from the Japanese* © All Rights Reserved by New
Directions Publishing Corporation, by permission of the publisher; A. D. Hope:
'The Gateway' from *Selected Poems* (Carcanet Press, 1986), by permission of the
publisher; Langston Hughes: 'The Negro Speaks of Rivers' from *The Collected
Poems of Langston Hughes* (Knopf, 1994), © 1994 by The Estate of Langston
Hughes, by permission of Alfred A. Knopf, a division of Random House Inc; Ted
Hughes: 'Full Moon and Little Frieda' from *Wodwo* (Faber & Faber, 1982);
Elizabeth Jennings: 'Into the Hour' from *New Collected Poems* (Carcanet Press,
2002); Donald Justice: 'Bus Stop' from *Selected Poems* (Anvil Press Poetry, 1980);
Patrick Kavanagh's 'Consider the Grass Growing' from *Collected Poems,* edited by
Antoinette Quinn (Allen Lane, 2004); Jane Kenyon: 'Let Evening Come' from
Otherwise: New and Selected Poems (Graywolf Press, 1996), © 1996 by Jane Kenyon;
Kesa'i: 'Flowers come as a gift', translated by Dick Davis, from *Borrowed Ware:
Medieval Persian Epigrams* (Anvil Press Poetry, 1996); Galway Kinnell: 'When one
has lived a long time alone' from *When One has Lived A Long Time Alone* (Knopf,
1990), © 1990 by Galway Kinnell, by permission of Alfred A. Knopf, a division of
Random House Inc; Philip Larkin: 'The Trees' from *Collected Poems* (Faber &
Faber, 1988); Dorianne Laux: 'Break' from *Awake* (University of Arkansas Press,
2001), © 2001 by Dorianne Laux; D. H. Lawrence: 'Trees in the Garden' from *The
Complete Poems of D. H. Lawrence* edited by V. de Sola Pinto and F. W. Roberts, ©
1964, 1971 by Angelo Ravagli and C. M. Weekley, Executors of the Estate of Frieda
Lawrence Ravagli, by permission of Viking Penguin, a division of Penguin Group
(USA) Inc; Giacomo Leopardi: 'To the Moon' translated by Eamon Grennan, from
Selected Poems (Princeton University Press, 1997); Michael Longley: 'Snow Water'
from *Snow Water* (Jonathan Cape, 2004), by permission of The Random House
Group Ltd; Norman MacCaig: Summer Farm, from *Collected Poems* (Chatto &
Windus, 1990); Louis MacNeice: 'Apple Blossom' from *Selected Poems* (Faber &
Faber, 1988), by permission of David Higham Associates; Derek Mahon:
'Everything is Going to be All Right' from *Collected Poems* (The Gallery Press,
1999), © 1999 by Derek Mahon, by kind permission of the author and The Gallery
Press, Loughcrew, Oldcastle, County Meath, Ireland; Charlotte Mew: 'In the Fields'
from *Collected Poems and Prose* edited by Val Warner (Carcanet Press, 1982), by
permission of the publisher; Marianne Moore: 'What Are Years' from *The Complete
Poems of Marianne Moore* (Faber & Faber, 1968); Marilyn Nelson: 'How I Discovered
Poetry' from *The Fields of Praise: New and Selected Poems* (Louisiana State
University Press, 1997), © 1997 by Marilyn Nelson; Pablo Neruda: 'Oh, Earth, Wait
for Me' translated by Alastair Reid, from *Isla Negra* (Souvenir Press, 1982),

Published by MQ Publications Limited
12 The Ivories, 6–8 Northampton Street
London N1 2HY
Tel: +44 (0) 20 7359 2244
Fax:+44 (0) 20 7359 1616
email: mail@mqpublications.com
website: www.mqpublications.com

ISBN: 1 84072 666 0

10 9 8 7 6 5 4 3 2 1

Printed and bound in China

Mimi Khalvati

Mimi Khalvati was born in Tehran, and grew up in England. She is founder of London's Poetry School and co-founded the Theater in Exile group. She has served as Poet in Residence at the Royal Mail, and worked as an actor and director in the UK and Iran.

She is a tutor at the internationally respected Arvon Foundation, and has taught creative writing at universities and colleges in the US and England.

Her poetry collections include *Persian Miniatures/A Belfast Kiss* (1990), *In White Ink* (1991), and *Mirrorwork* (1995) which received an Arts Council of England Writers' Award. *Entries on Light* appeared in 1997, and *Selected Poems* in 2000. Her collection *The Chine* was published in 2002. She also co-edited *Tying the Song: A First Anthology from the Poetry School 1997–2000* (2000) and *Entering the Tapestry: A Second Anthology from the Poetry School* (2003).